THE ART of
LOVING GOD

Art is the acco

JANE STANTON

Julie Ackerman Link

The Art of Loving God

© 2003 Julie Ackerman Link

Discovery House Publishers is affiliated with RBC Ministries, Grand
Rapids, Michigan 49501.

Cover Photos: Index Stock (inset); Pictorial Archive (background)

Printed in the United States of America

03 04 05 06 07 08 09 10 / CHG / 10 9 8 7 6 5 4 3 2 1

Introduction

When God in His fiery presence descended from heaven to meet Moses on Mount Sinai, He delivered a document citing ten basic rules for His people to live by, the most important being "You shall have no other gods before me."

This statement was revolutionary. All other nations worshiped many gods. But God's chosen people, the children of Israel, were to establish a nation that would be a light to the world, revealing to all others the joy that comes when people live in accord with the design and purpose of our loving Creator, the one true God, who formed us in His own image.

Years later, Moses explained the first commandment. Having no other god but God means loving Him with every aspect of our being—heart, soul, and strength (Deuteronomy 6:5). Jesus affirmed this interpretation (Mark 12:30). To love God means having a relationship with Him that is so full and satisfying that it slowly crowds out all competing desires, identifications, thoughts, or actions.

Since the day God delivered the first hand-carved edition of the document now popularly called "The Ten Commandments," sculptors, calligraphers, and designers have formed those words into works of art. But God's intent was not that we would shape the words into ornate decorations. He wants the words to shape us. When God's law of love becomes part of our internal makeup rather than something we simply quote or use as ornamentation, our lives become the unique piece of artwork He designed each of us to be.

The Art of Loving God is not about creating something beautiful for God; it's about allowing God to re-create in us the beauty He originally formed. It's there, just waiting to be recognized, restored, and made real.

I LOVE ART FAIRS. I go to admire the creativity of the artists, to get ideas for things I might be able to make, and to buy things to decorate my house and surround myself with beauty.

At the last art fair I attended, however, I found something to decorate my lapel rather than my home. And in this particular case, I was intrigued with the item not for its beauty but for its meaning.

The pin I found featured the faces of three characters from *The Wonderful Wizard of Oz*: the Cowardly Lion, the Tin Woodman, and the Scarecrow.

Dangling beneath the face of the friendly but Cowardly Lion is a yellow star with the words "Be Brave." Beneath the hollow stare of the Tin Woodman dangles a red heart with the words "Have a Heart." And beneath the mindless expression of the Scarecrow is a turquoise circle with the words "Use Your Brain."

The artist was memorializing L. Frank Baum's childhood classic, but to me the pin was a symbol of what Jews call the Shema, and what Jesus called the Greatest Commandment.

When Moses addressed a throng of six million recently freed slaves after being called by God to lead them out of Egyptian captivity, he began with these words:

> Hear, O Israel: The Lord our God, the Lord is one. Love the Lord your God with all your heart and with all your soul and with all your strength.   —Deuteronomy 6:4–5

Thousands of years later, Jewish religious leaders asked Jesus, "What is the most important commandment?"

He answered by quoting Moses:

The most important one is this: "Hear, O Israel, the Lord our God, the Lord is one. Love the Lord your God with all your heart and with all your soul and with all your mind and with all your strength."   —Mark 12:29–30

If I hadn't been studying the Greatest Commandment just before attending the art fair, I might not have recognized any spiritual lesson in the pin. But my new mindset gave me a new perspective on the characters. I saw the Tin Woodman who finally feels emotion as a symbol of loving God with my heart. I saw the Scarecrow who finds out that he can think as a symbol of loving God with my mind. And I saw the Cowardly Lion

Love cannot survive if you just give it scraps of yourself, scraps of your time, scraps of your thoughts.

MARY O'HARA

who finds courage as a symbol of loving God with my strength.

I bought the pin and now wear it to remind myself that to live the way God intended, I need to love God in all of these areas of my life. The trouble with the pin, however, or any symbol, for that matter, is that it has no value if no one understands what it represents. So the big question is: What on earth does it mean to love God with my heart, soul, mind, and strength? And how can I do it if I don't even know what it means?

Years ago in an editorial meeting, one of the writers told of a time when she had admitted to an older, mature Christian that she wasn't sure what it meant to love God. She described the look of disdain and disbelief that she received in return for her confession and said that it kept her from ever again admitting such a thing—until that moment in our meeting.

We went around the table asking ourselves the question. Even though we all had positions of leadership in our churches and other religious organizations, none of us did a very good job of articulating what it means to love God.

The Meaning of Love

What is the meaning of this mysterious four-letter verb/noun that we use to describe everything from the absurd to the sacred, from feelings to actions, from preferences to passions? How is it that I use the same word to express fondness for art fairs, Mexican food, and even my dog as I do for God? To be honest, there are many times when my use of the word *love* is more sincere when I'm referring to the animal who worships me than the God I claim to worship.

Everyone admits that love is wonderful and necessary, yet no one can agree on what it is.

DIANE ACKERMAN

Part of the problem may be the word itself. The Hebrew Old Testament and the Greek New Testament both have more than one word that is translated *love* in the English Bible. But my English dictionary lists twenty-one definitions of love. When a single word has so many meanings, it's no wonder we have so much confusion about it.

The Eskimos had fifty two names for snow because snow was important to them; there ought to be as many for love.

MARGARET ATWOOD

We can easily describe what it feels like to "be loved," but we have trouble translating that into what it means to "be loving." We feel loved when someone wants to be with us, takes the risk of letting us know him, takes the time to get to know us, and always does what is in our best interest. Our desire to be on the receiving end of this kind of devotion is much greater than our ability to return it.

To be loved is one of the strongest of all desires. The need for love is as much a part of God's design for humans as the need for air, water, and food. We can't lead a healthy life without it. Sadly, however, humans have managed to thoroughly mess up God's distribution system. One of the ways God passes along His love is through others, generally those closest to us. Children learn to love by being loved by moms and dads, grandpas and grandmas, aunts and uncles.

The birthday card I bought for my mother this year was short and simple. It read, "Before I knew anything else, I knew how it felt to be loved. Thanks, Mom. Happy Birthday."

I have always taken for granted the love of my parents, but over the years I've been surprised and saddened to learn how many people have not enjoyed this blessing.

Melissa is one of the extreme cases. From as early as she can remember, her parents treated her as if she were less than human. During the day, she was locked in a closet. At mealtime, she was taken outside on a leash and made to eat on the porch. Relatives called her "it." The only emotion Melissa ever felt was anger, so that was what she expressed. At age twelve, she was finally removed from her abusive family by child protective services, but in every foster family her behavior remained the same—rage and violence—even toward those who truly wanted to help her. As a last resort, she was placed in a Christian residential care center for troubled children. Within a year Melissa's heart began to soften. From people who were kind to her, she learned how to express kindness. Eventually, she turned her life over to God because she had experienced His love through the care and concern of godly counselors and staff. Melissa came to love God because God's people loved her.

Those of us who have grown up in loving homes may be more willing to trust love than Melissa, but we may also be more likely to believe lies about love. We grow up believing the romanticized definition—that being in love means always feeling passion. We disregard those who tell us that loving another human being is difficult work that requires knowledge, skill, and perseverance to go along with emotion. By focusing on the emotion and neglecting the behavior, we make ourselves vulnerable

Few people know what they mean when they say, "I love you." . . . Well, what does the word love mean? It means total interest. I think the reason very few people really fall in love with anyone is they're not willing to pay the price. The price is you have to adjust yourself to them.

KATHARINE HEPBURN

to all kinds of false expressions of love. Our imperfect understanding makes us prone to being deceived as well as to being deceptive.

So how can we learn the sacred meaning of a word that has been twisted and distorted by overuse and misuse?

The Bible describes love in this familiar New Testament passage:

> Love is patient, love is kind. It does not envy, it does not boast, it is not proud. It is not rude, it is not self-seeking, it is not easily angered, it keeps no record of wrongs. Love does not delight in evil but rejoices with the truth. It always protects, always trusts, always hopes, always perseveres.
>
> —1 Corinthians 13:4–7

In other words, love seeks the highest good. God's love is perfect because He seeks the highest good for all creation. Every human being longs to be the recipient of this kind of love, but no human can provide it. The only place to experience genuine love is in a relationship with the One whose very being defines it. Not only is God the perfect example of love, He *is* love, and apart from His love for us none of us could love or be loved (1 John 4:19).

In real love you want the other person's good. In romantic love you want the other person.

MARGARET ANDERSON

The Call of Love

But how does God love us? The apostle John gives the answer in his letter to first-century believers:

> This is how God showed his love among us:
> He sent his one and only Son into the world
> that we might live through him.   —1 John 4:9

Beginning with Adam and Eve, God has been making it His top priority to establish a relationship with the people He created—first one couple, then one family, then one nation, and now the world. God wants to bring everyone into His family by reconciling the world to Himself through His Son. (See 2 Corinthians 5:18–19.) To do so, He expresses His love with His heart, soul, mind, and strength. In other words, God asks of us only what He first demonstrated to us! We learn to love God by discovering how He loves us.

God Loves Us with His Heart

By Wanting a Relationship with Us

We often misunderstand the role of feelings, emotion, and desire in regard to love. Some of us exaggerate the importance of these three while others prefer to disregard them because of the confusion and complexity they add to relationships. But they are a legitimate part of love, and God's love for us involves all three. Moses assures us that God feels compassion for us and is slow to become angry (Exodus 34:6). The prophet Zephaniah said that God "delights" in us (3:17). And Jesus, at the last Passover meal, prayed, "Father, I want those you have given me to be with me where I am" (John 17:24). From these and many more Scripture passages, we learn that God's love involves the way He feels about us, not just the way He acts toward us.

Do you remember your "first love" and the feelings associated with it—the awareness that someone you liked also liked you and found you delightful and desirable?

Imagine that someone being God!

> The Lord your God is with you, he is mighty to save. He will take great delight in you, he will quiet you with his love, he will rejoice over you with singing.
>
> ZEPHANIAH 3:17

God Loves Us with His Soul

By Revealing Himself to Us

Only the last book of the Bible is titled "Revelation," but all of Scripture *is* revelation. All sixty-six books are a record of God's many attempts to let Himself be known by those He created. (See Amos 4:13; Isaiah 43:10.) Think about how special you feel when someone trusts you enough to tell you his secrets.

Imagine that someone being God!

God Loves Us with His Mind

By Knowing Who We Are and What We Need

No loving parent expects a toddler to mow the lawn, repair the car, or fix meals. Likewise, God does not expect His children to perform tasks beyond their ability. Because He made us, He knows our limitations. "As a father has compassion on his children, so the Lord has compassion on those who fear him; for he knows how we are formed, he remembers that we are dust" (Psalm 103:13–14).

A loving relationship with God does not begin by figuring out what He wants us to do for Him but by realizing what He has done, is doing, and wants to do for us.

Have you ever had someone come alongside you and say, "You're having a hard time with that, aren't you? Here, let me do it for you"?

Imagine that someone being God!

God Loves Us with His Strength
By Giving Us What Is Good

"Don't take candy from strangers." Behind this timeless warning is the knowledge that evil, to get what it wants, must disguise itself as something desirable. Like a pedophile who poses as someone who is kind and generous, Satan masquerades as the one giving out all the goodies. But the "gifts" of Satan are all counterfeits. They lead to futility, despair, and uselessness.

The gifts of God, on the other hand, lead to purpose, meaning, and fruitfulness (James 1:16–18).

> Love is that which exists to do good, not merely to get good.
>
> VICTORIA WOODHULL

Loving parents don't indulge a child's every craving, but they eagerly and joyfully supply every need. Parents give many additional gifts as well, not to bribe children or lure them for some selfish purpose, but because they love to see their children happy.

Being loved means having someone know us so well and care about us so much that he uses all his strength to give us what is good and do what is best

20

for us even before we ask, even when we don't know what it is.

Imagine that someone being God!

As perfect as God's love is, however, we will be dissatisfied if we simply receive it and don't return it. To be complete, love must flow in two directions. It must be received *and* reciprocated. Therefore, God's call "of" love is paired with His command "to" love.

The Command To Love

All the love in the world cannot satisfy us if we receive it but refuse to give it.

> Love has nothing to do with what you are expecting to get—only what you are expecting to give—which is everything. What you will receive in return varies. But it really has no connection with what you give. You give because you love and cannot help giving. If you are very lucky, you may be loved back. That is delicious, but it does not necessarily happen.
>
> KATHARINE HEPBURN

Love is not a cup or a pail or a reservoir that we can fill. It's a river that flows from God to us and back to God again through our love for other people. Jesus said,

> "Whoever welcomes one of these little children
> in my name welcomes me; and whoever welcomes
> me does not welcome me but the one who
> sent me."   —Mark 9:37

Our willingness to love others affects our ability to feel loved. In fact, if we refuse to love, eventually we will feel unloved. God's people drifted away from Him not because He stopped loving them, but because they stopped "feeling loved" when they stopped loving the Giver of good things and started loving His gifts instead.

The desire to be loved is not wrong. God Himself wants to be loved, so much so that He made it the most important commandment, as the Shema states and as Jesus confirmed. And contrary to what I thought for many years, God did not leave us in the dark as to what it means to love Him, nor does He make us guess how He wants to be loved. In fact, He didn't just tell us, He showed us! God wants us to love Him in the same way He loves us—with every desire and feeling, with every aspect of our being, with every thought, and with everything we do.

Loving God with All My Heart

Does It Matter What I Want?

Snacking on the forbidden fruit was Eve's first sin, but the act itself had roots in desire. Sin started growing in Eve's heart when she wanted something God didn't want her to have. That may be why the curse on Eve involves desire. According to Genesis 3:16, her "desire" will be for her husband. Reading this in the context of twentieth-century western middle-class culture, some have concluded that it means women will desire man's authority. But when we look at it in light of male-female relationships throughout history, a different picture emerges.

In most cultures, women have remained voluntarily subservient (not to be mistaken with submissive) to men. They desire to have a man who will protect them and take care of them. Recently, a highly educated young woman I know was re-thinking the Western practice of dating and marriage. "Forget this 'love is all we need' stuff," she said. "I want security." Unfortunately, some men exploit this desire and use it to "rule over" women in ways that God never intended.

A problem among women today is that they want a man—any man—at any cost. But not all males become good men, and not many females are taught to recognize the difference. Women who desire a man more than they desire God are courting trouble for themselves and for their offspring.

But desire is not bad. It is part of our emotional makeup that God established at creation. Our desires work in conjunction with feelings and emotions to stimulate, energize, and enable us to experience life to the fullest extent. Our own feelings and desires help us understand the part of God's character that is emotional. When desire is satisfied, we feel good, at least temporarily; when it's not, we feel bad. To maintain good feelings, we need to align our desires with God's. That's where Eve went wrong.

Eve allowed Satan to seduce her and plant within her the seed of desire for knowledge God didn't want her to have. And that started the downward plunge. At Satan's prompting, Eve began doubting God's love for her (which is where sin often begins). She began questioning whether God had her best interests or His own in mind when He set limits on the food she could eat and the knowledge she could have.

Satan is no creative genius, but he's an expert at creating doubt. Since his initial success with Eve, he has continued practicing on all of us. The lie that Satan tells over and over again is that God is the enemy, that he is stingy, and that he will keep us from getting what we need, want, and deserve. Satan takes advantage of our need for love by making us feel as if God's love is insufficient. Then he slithers in to tempt us with tasty counterfeits.

Satan would have us believe that we have no control over our feelings, desires, and emotions—that they come to us uninvited and that we are powerless to change them or make them leave. But he is wrong. It isn't easy, but we can learn to love and choose what is good for us emotionally just as we do in the physical realm with food and exercise.

Flee the evil desires of youth, and pursue righteousness, faith, love and peace, along with those who call on the Lord out of a pure heart.

2 TIMOTHY 2:22

When I love God with all my heart, my desires match His. I want what He wants and what He says is good. I feel the way He feels about good and evil.

Loving God with all my heart answers the question "Where did I come from?" *I came from God, and all my needs and desires are ultimately met and satisfied in Him alone.*

Questions to ask myself . . .

- *What are my strongest desires?*

- *How do I satisfy my desires?*

- *Do I violate any of God's commands in my attempts to get what I want?*

- *How do my feelings about God affect my desires?*

- *What do I want that God doesn't want me to have?*

- *Do I believe that God wants to give me what is good?*

Loving God with All My Soul

Does It Matter Who I Am?

The Hebrew word translated "soul" in Shema (Deuteronomy 6:5) means "breath," which is what God breathed into Adam to change him from an elaborate dustball to a living being (Genesis 2:7).

The Greek word translated "soul" in Mark 12:30 is *psuche*, from which we get the word psychology. *Psuche* is also the word that is translated "life" in these well-known verses:

> Whoever finds his life will lose it, and whoever loses his life for my sake will find it.
>
> —Matthew 10:39

> For whoever wants to save his life will lose it, but whoever loses his life for me will find it.
>
> —Matthew 16:25

A word that might give us a better understanding of this concept is "self." *Psuche* is what makes each of us unique, what sets us apart from everyone else. It's the essence of our identity. So Jesus is saying that we need to give up our "selves."

Women are generally good at this. We seem to have an innate ability to give up our selves, but it's what we give ourselves up to that causes problems. In adolescence and early adulthood, we give ourselves to the boys we like. To get them to notice us, we devote our time and attention to whatever they spend their time on whether or not it's of any interest to us. Advice columnists encourage this by telling young girls to show interest in what boys are interested in. That's not bad advice; it's the polite thing to do in any relationship.

She tried to be somebody by trying to be like everybody and became a nobody.

UNKNOWN

But women, especially younger ones, take this to unhealthy extremes. In college, I spent a whole year "volunteering" in a greenhouse because my boyfriend was doing graduate work at the Tree Research Center. I gained a love for all things green and growing, but I lost valuable time by neglecting my own God-given interests and abilities. (I also lost a lot of fingernails planting walnut trees!)

> You can't make someone love you, but you can make yourself into someone who can be loved.
>
> UNKNOWN

Later in life, women give themselves up to their husbands, children, or careers, depending on which "track" they choose. I'm not implying that any of these is a bad choice. But we need to keep reminding ourselves that they all hold an inherent danger: each of them can take the place of God in our lives. Anything—even good things—that becomes a substitute for God is an idol. Idolatry in any form is sin, but when children become an idol the dangerous consequences are multiplied and magnified. Not only are we neglecting our own souls, but we are endangering the souls of our children because we are communicating to them that they are more important than God.

Secular psychologists make a lot of money promising to help people "find themselves." Biblical psychologists know that the only place to find ourselves is in God. Knowing this, think how dangerous it is to give the care of our souls over to someone who does not believe in God, much less know Him.

Ironically, the only way any of us ever find ourselves is to lose ourselves in God, for that is where we find our true selves—the selves we are meant to be.

The French use the phrase *raison d'être*, which means

"reason for being." Loving God with my soul means embracing the truth that my reason for being on earth is to become all that God created me to be—not what my parents dreamed I would become nor what my spouse or children or friends tell me I should be. To do this, I must know God so well that I trust Him to reveal my unique abilities and passions and to lead me to the place where I can use them to the fullest extent possible in the way that will bring the most glory to Him.

I have a long way to go in this regard. Instead of losing myself in God, I often find myself trying to impress people. Raised by Christian parents who were active in our local church, I have been blessed by numerous godly influences in my life. Thus I have a good understanding of the right things to do. After years of practice, I can often get myself to do good things. But I know how often I am doing them for the wrong reasons—to please people, to make myself look good, to elevate myself above others.

This is no minor flaw. It's the sin that Jesus condemned so harshly in some of the religious leaders of His day. People admired the Pharisees for their knowledge of Scripture and their meticulous keeping of the law. But their motives let off such a stench that Jesus compared them to whitewashed coffins. They did everything outwardly to make themselves look good, but their inner selves were like rotting flesh. They appeared to be the epitome of righteousness, but they were preaching from atop a landfill of their own self-righteousness. Those who had lived their whole lives "in the neighborhood" didn't

> True love isn't the kind that endures through long years of absence, but the kind that endures through long years of propinquity.
>
> HELEN ROWLAND

smell anything foul because it was the only "air" they had ever breathed. But Jesus, having just come from heaven, immediately recognized the stench of spiritual death. The Pharisees weren't loving God with their soul by giving glory to God with every ounce of their being; they were gaining glory for themselves.

In stark contrast to the Pharisees stands Mary the mother of Jesus, a young woman who loved God with all her soul. Upon learning that she had been chosen to give birth to the Messiah, Mary submitted herself to God with a statement that both startles and convicts me every time I read it. Her story has become trivialized in countless Christmas pageants, so we have to strain to hear the quiet passion in her response to the angel Gabriel when he visited her one ordinary day and gave her this extraordinary news:

"You will be with child and give birth to a son,

and you are to give him the name Jesus. He
will be great and will be called the Son of the
Most High. The Lord God will give him the
throne of his father David, and he will reign
over the house of Jacob forever; his kingdom
will never end. . . . The Holy Spirit will come
upon you, and the power of the Most High
will overshadow you. So the holy one to be
born will be called the Son of God."

—Luke 1:31–35

Mary didn't run to her mother or girlfriends to get
advice about what she should do. She didn't turn to her
father or fiancé to ask permission to give an answer.
Instead, even though she must have known that disbelief,
ridicule, and scorn would follow her all the days of her life,
Mary uttered the words that always get stuck in my throat:

"I am the Lord's servant. May it be to me as you have said" (Luke 1:38).

By losing herself in God, Mary found her true identity as the mother of God's Son, the world's Savior. In so doing, she gave us another gift: a timeless example of what it means to love God with all our souls.

Loving God with all my soul answers the question "Who am I?" *I am a one-of-a-kind person made in God's image with unique talents and abilities, passions and motives, opportunities and experiences, that are best used to glorify God and further His kingdom.*

Questions to ask myself . . .

- *What talents and abilities do I have?*

- *What passions motivate me?*

- *What mix of qualities and abilities makes me unique?*

- *Am I listening to God tell me who I am or to others tell me who I should be?*

Loving God with All My Mind

Does It Matter What I Think?

I doubt if Mary would have made the decision to say yes to Gabriel had she not known God and the Scriptures. For Mary to submit herself to this life-altering call, she had to want God's will more than her own way. She had to believe that God loved her and wanted what was good for her. She had to know that God's purpose was better than her plan. She must have believed the writings of King Solomon: "In his heart a man plans his course, but the Lord determines his steps" (Proverbs 16:9). "Many are the plans in a man's heart, but it is the Lord's purpose that prevails" (Proverbs 19:21).

Earlier I said that Satan planted within Eve the seed of desire for knowledge that God didn't want her to have. Eve's desire for knowledge was not bad, but the knowledge of evil was something that God wanted to keep to Himself. Creation was good, and He wanted to keep it that way. But Eve introduced evil into our lives and made it necessary for us to learn to distinguish good from evil.

We tend to think that evil should be obvious, but it's not because it masquerades as good. The book of Hebrews confirms that learning to tell the difference requires more than a weekend seminar: "[S]olid food is for the mature, who by constant use have trained themselves to distinguish good from evil" (5:14).

> Conscience is what hurts when all your other parts feel good.
>
> UNKNOWN

God's desire to keep us from knowing evil wasn't just a hopeful plan for the past that died with Eve's disobedience; it is still God's will and part of His plan for the future. Writing to the church in Rome, Paul encouraged believers to return

to the way God intended His people to be: "I want you to
be wise about what is good, and innocent about what is evil"
(Romans 16:19). This is a difficult assignment in
a world that assaults us with images of evil

parading as good, but it's one that we need
to take seriously.

To discern good from evil, truth
from lies, wholesome beauty from physical
attractiveness, and genuine love from lonely
neediness, we need to know what God says about
these things. We need to have clear thinking and solid
beliefs.

Scripture memorializes two women for their thoughts.
One has become an example of doubt, the other of faith.

In Genesis, we read about Sarah, who laughed in disbelief
after hearing an angel tell her husband that she was going to

become a mother at an age when most women were already enjoying grandchildren or great grandchildren:

> So Sarah laughed to herself as she thought,
> "After I am worn out and my master is old, will
> I now have this pleasure?"—Genesis 18:12

Ironically, the wife of the man known as "the father of faith" (Romans 4:12–13) is remembered for her doubt. She didn't believe that God could fulfill a promise which experience told her was impossible.

In the Gospels, we read about another woman who, like Sarah, had waited for many years to have a desire satisfied. She, however, had kept her faith.

> [S]he thought, "If I just touch his clothes, I
> will be healed."   —Mark 5:28

After twelve years of going from doctor to doctor only to get sicker and poorer, this anonymous woman had the faith to believe that a rabbi could do for her what doctors could not. Instead of building her belief system on the foundation of her own disappointing experiences, she built it on her knowledge of the proclamations of ancient Jewish prophets who predicted that the Messiah would come with healing.

In her book *When Life and Beliefs Collide*, Carolyn Custis James confirms the importance of women having knowledge and theological understanding:

> [A] woman's interest in theology ought to be the first thing to catch a man's eye. A wife's theology should be what a husband prizes most about her. He may always enjoy her cooking and cherish her gentle ways, but in the intensity of battle, when adversity flattens him or he faces an insurmountable challenge, she is the soldier nearest him, and it is her

theology that he will hear. A woman's theology
suddenly matters when a man is facing a
crisis and she is the only one around to offer
encouragement (p. 51).

Loving God with my mind means knowing the pattern
of God's relationship with humanity: revelation, alienation,
reconciliation. The pattern started with Creation, the Fall,
and the giving of the Law. It continued in the Incarnation,
the Crucifixion, and the Resurrection. And it keeps repeating
itself in individual lives on a daily basis. God gives us life
and breath, sunshine and rain, food and flowers, sunsets
and sunrises, friends and family. Yet we are constantly
enticed to pursue things that look nicer, smell sweeter, or
promise something better.

Whenever I speak at writers' or editors' conferences, I
close with one of my favorite verses:

Finally, brothers [and sisters], whatever is true, whatever is noble, whatever is right, whatever is pure, whatever is lovely, whatever is admirable—if anything is excellent or praiseworthy—think about such things.

—Philippians 4:8

Turned into questions, the verse is a good way to evaluate what we write and publish. It's also an excellent way to test my thoughts: Are they true? Are they noble? Are they right? Are they pure? Are they lovely? Are they admirable? When I ask myself those questions before opening my mouth or closing my mind, I wind up in a lot less trouble.

When I love God with my mind, I agree with Him about what is good. I reconcile my thoughts to His until I think what He thinks. I agree with Him about the way things are, the way things should be, and what He wants me to do about it.

Loving God with my mind answers the question "Why am I here?" *I am here to know God, to enjoy His company and the beauty of His creation, and to participate with Him in the most important work of all—redemption—as He patiently and lovingly brings all creation into reconciliation with Himself through increased knowledge of good and innocence of evil.*

Questions to ask myself . . .

- *What thoughts guide me? Are they true? How do I know?*

- *Do I think my way to decisions or just do whatever "feels" right?*

- *Do I think about the right way to respond to situations, or do I just react on impulse?*

- *Does my thinking lead to solutions or problems?*

- *Am I more curious about good or evil? Am I more drawn to good or evil? Why?*

Loving God with All My Strength

Does It Matter What I Do?

On the morning of September 11, 2001, I had just finished reading the book of Esther for my devotions when I learned what was happening in New York City.

I didn't immediately see the relationship between the events that I'd just read about and those that I was watching on a small screen in my living room. But as the day and week progressed, I realized that the story of the Persian queen was like a 2500-year foreshadowing of the day we will always remember as 9/11.

The book of Esther tells the story of a young Jewish orphan who became queen of Persia, much of which is now Iraq and Iran.

Imagine being a young girl in Esther's position. Not only was she living in the capitol of the world's most powerful nation; she also was living in the palace of the world's most powerful ruler. Esther was living a familiar female fantasy. She was the wife of the most powerful man in the world. But then imagine having the cousin who raised you interrupt your privileged life to inform you that the fate of all your relatives depended on your willingness to risk your life by confronting your ruthless husband.

Would you risk losing your position of power, prestige, and comfort—perhaps even your life—to prevent a tragedy that seemed so unlikely to happen? Or would you rationalize that you could do more good for more people by staying alive than by dying? Mordecai spoke forcefully to his cousin

> Character cannot be developed in ease and quiet. Only through experience of trial and suffering can the soul be strengthened, vision cleared, ambition inspired, and success achieved.
>
> HELEN KELLER

with words that may have sounded like this: "Listen, Esther, don't think for a minute that all of this good fortune has happened to you simply for your pleasure. And don't be so foolish as to think that you will be spared just because you're living in the king's palace. If you don't save your people, God will, but no one will save you. And who knows, perhaps you've been put in this position for the sole purpose of doing what needs to be done today—saving the lives of your people."

Worry does not empty tomorrow of its sorrow. It empties today of its strength.

CORRIE TEN BOOM

After fasting and praying for three days, Esther accepted the challenge and risked her life by appealing to the king, who then spared the lives of all the exiled Jews living in the Persian Empire.

As I listened to the stories of the phone calls made by

people on United Airlines flight 93 that crashed in Pennsylvania, I thought, "That plane must have had some Esthers onboard." They heard the call, recognized their duty, and risked their own lives to save others.

Then I thought: If God had people onboard that plane to thwart the enemy, why would He not have had people in other strategic places who could have stopped the evil of that day before it got so big and so ugly?

I think He did. I believe God had people stationed at all kinds of intersections along the way, who, for one reason or another, took the easy way and turned their heads, ignored the evidence, and refused to believe that anything bad would happen if they ignored "potential" evil. How could they have known that taking the easy way on that day would lead to death for so many innocent people? How could they have known that ignoring a small suspicion would result in evil on a scale that the Western world seldom sees?

This, of course, leads to more personal questions: How much evil do I ignore in my own life because I refuse to believe that my anger, habit, or rebellion will ever hurt anyone, or will ever get so big that I can't control it? And how much evil do I ignore in other people because I am too much of a coward to try to stop it, or because I don't want anyone to dislike me, or because I don't want to be inconvenienced?

As I witnessed the unfolding drama of 9/11, I saw my own "call to love" in a new way. As Mordecai said to Esther, "Don't think you're here simply for your own pleasure and enjoyment; you're here to stand against evil."

Whenever evil rears its ugly head, the world asks: Where is God?

Jesus told us where God is. Speaking to the disciples, He said: "Before long, the world will not see me anymore, but you will see me. Because I live, you also will live. On that day, you will realize that I am in my Father, and you are in me, and I am in you" (John 14:19–20).

We can ignore the question people are asking. We can shrug our shoulders and even join those who are asking it. Or we can say, "Here He is, living in me. In the power of Christ, I'm standing against evil. Will you join me?"

Loving God with our strength involves more than filling our calendars with charitable activities or checking off a list of good deeds. It means daily doing right in the little things that are difficult so that when a

> If I put my own good name before the other's highest good, then I know nothing of Calvary love.
>
> AMY CARMICHAEL

"big" opportunity comes along we won't have to waste time figuring out what right is.

Loving God with my strength means having the courage to risk my "self" for the sake of what I know is true and right and good.

Loving God with all my strength answers the question "Where am I going?" *I am going where God leads. I may not know ahead of time where that will be, but I know He will not lead me along the path of least resistance, for He wants me to become strong so that when I am called into action I will be ready to carry the light of His truth, goodness, and love into dark places where evil is causing chaos and confusion.*

Questions to ask myself . . .

- *What am I trying to accomplish?*

- *How do I get it done?*

- *Do I take the easy way or the right way?*

- *What actions characterize me?*

- *What am I uniquely qualified to do or in a unique position to accomplish?*

Love Never Fails

OCTOBER 8, 2002 | Curators at New York's Metropolitan Museum of Art are mourning the fall of Adam. In fact, the tragedy has brought them to their knees. No, they're not repenting of the sin that started in the Garden of Eden with the fall of the first Adam. They're lamenting the plunge of a priceless fifteenth-century sculpture from its pedestal, and they're on their knees picking up the fragments.

When the statue fell, it didn't break into nice neat pieces. The arms, legs, and head weren't separated from the torso in such a way that they could be glued back together neatly and easily. In the words of the restorer, part of Adam was "pulverized." Experts predict that it will take two years to piece Adam together again, but they promise he'll be almost as good as new when he's returned to public view.

Imagine if you were given the dust and particles of Adam and were told to put him back together again. If you're like me, you'd rather leave that task to experts.

That's a small example of what we attempt to do whenever we try to "restore" ourselves from the effects of the Fall. Like the statue, the original Adam and everyone after him have been shattered and pulverized by sin, but we did not break into pieces that can be easily identified as emotions, personality, mind, and body. We all lie in a pile of dust and broken body parts on the floor of creation. And we have only one hope for wholeness—the One who created us is the only One with the knowledge and skill to put us back together.

In a letter to Christians living in Asia Minor (now Turkey), the apostle Paul disclosed the bonding agent that Jesus uses to restore us to our original glory:

> Therefore, as God's chosen people, holy and
> dearly loved, clothe yourselves with compassion,
> kindness, humility, gentleness and patience. Bear
> with each other and forgive whatever grievances
> you may have against one another. Forgive as
> the Lord forgave you. And over all these virtues
> put on love, which binds them all together in
> perfect unity.   —Colossians 3:12–14

In another letter, this one to Christians living in Corinth, Paul wrote "Love never fails" (1 Corinthians 13:8). If that is so, why did love fail to keep sin from entering the Garden of Eden? If love never fails, where does all the hate come from? What are the answers to the questions so many people keep asking when terrible things happen: How can God be good and yet allow so much evil? How can He be all-powerful and yet do nothing to stop all the suffering?

How can He be the full expression of love and yet tolerate so much hate?

When we consider the options available to God, we realize that He made the most loving choice of all in giving us the freedom to reject Him, which, when we do, means opening the door for evil. For love to exist, rejection must be an option. Love is not love if no choice is involved. In fact, it is our freedom that proves how much God really does love us. For a god who forced himself on us would be a rapist, not a lover. A god who stood over us with a clenched fist would be a tyrant, not a loving father. And a god who constrained us to do good would be a slave driver, not a savior.

That we ought to love Him we are never in doubt, but whether we do love Him, we may well begin to question. A deep yearning in our innermost being "to know Him more clearly, love Him more dearly and follow Him more nearly" is probably all to which we dare lay claim.

HELEN ROSEVEARE

Instead of using force to hold us, God relies on the splendor of His love to attract us. In extravagant expressions of truth, goodness, and beauty He woos us so that we'll desire Him. But then He waits for us to choose Him. This freedom is the ultimate expression of love.

I started with three characters from *The Wonderful Wizard of Oz* who represent three of the ways we're to love God. But what about Dorothy? Does she represent anything in the metaphor? At first I wasn't sure, but I'm beginning to see that Dorothy represents loving God with my soul. Throughout the story, Dorothy wants only one thing—to go home. And isn't that what we all want, really?

We all want to find the place where we belong. We want to find a family who loves us. If we grew up in a loving home, we try to re-create it or return to it. If we grew up in a not-so-loving home, we try to replace it with something better. But we all keep searching for the place where we know we are loved, where we can let down our guard without losing our safety—in other words, the place where we can rest.

A songwriter who was also ancient Israel's greatest king knew the location of that place: "My soul finds rest in God alone; my salvation comes from him" (Psalm 62:1). The Roman emperor Augustine, in the opening of his Confessions, alluded to this psalm when he wrote:

> Can any praise be worthy of the Lord's majesty?
> How magnificent his strength! How inscrutable
> his wisdom! Man is one of your creatures,
> Lord, and his instinct is to praise you. He
> bears about him the mark of death, the sign of

his own sin, to remind him that you thwart the proud. But still, since he is a part of your creation, he wishes to praise you. The thought of you stirs him so deeply that he cannot be content unless he praises you, because you made us for yourself and our hearts find no peace until they rest in you. —Book 1

We all want to go home, but many of us spend our lives trying to find the place without realizing that we first need to find the person—the Father—the one who created home, who knows where home is, and who keeps calling us to come and enjoy His wonderful company.

And what do all the great words come to in the end, but that?—I love you—I am at rest with you—I have come home.

DOROTHY L. SAYERS